Copyright © 2023 by Herman Strange (Author)

All rights reserved. This book or any portion thereof may not be reproduced or used in any manner whatsoever without the express written permission of the publisher except for the use of brief quotations in a book review.

This book is copyright protected. This is only for personal use. You cannot amend, distributor, sell, use, quote or paraphrase any part or the content within this book without the consent of the author. Please note the information contained within this document is for educational and entertainment purposes only. Every attempt has been made to provide accurate, up to date and reliable complete information. No warranties of any kind are expressed or implied.

Readers acknowledge that the author is not engaging in the rendering of legal, financial, medical or professional advice. The content of this book has been derived from various sources. Please consult a licensed professional before attempting any techniques outlined in this book.

By reading this document, the readers agree that under no circumstances are the author responsible for any losses, direct or indirect, which are incurred as a result of the use of information contained within this document, including but not limited to errors, omissions or inaccuracies.

Thank you very much for reading this book.

AI-Driven Crypto Investing
Subtitle: Strategies for Maximizing Rewards and Minimizing Risks in the Volatile Cryptocurrency Market

Series: Rise of Cognitive Computing: AI Evolution from Origins to Adoption
Author: Herman Strange

Table of Contents

Introduction 6

Brief history of cryptocurrency and its evolution to the present day 6

Importance of AI in financial decision making 9

How AI is changing the way we invest in cryptocurrencies 12

Chapter 1: Understanding the Crypto Market 15

Satoshi Nakamoto's whitepaper and the birth of Bitcoin 15

How blockchain technology works and its potential applications 18

Market capitalization and volatility in the cryptocurrency market 21

Regulatory and legal considerations for cryptocurrency investing 24

Chapter 2: Introduction to AI-Driven Crypto Investing 27

Machine learning and deep learning algorithms used in cryptocurrency investing 27

Sentiment analysis and natural language processing for analyzing news and social media 30

Cryptocurrency trading bots and their capabilities 33

Hybrid approaches to investing using both AI and human decision-making 37

Chapter 3: Pitfalls and Risks of AI-Driven Crypto Investing 43

    Confirmation bias and other cognitive biases that can affect algorithmic decision-making 43

    The importance of monitoring and adjusting algorithms in response to changing market conditions 46

    The potential for AI-driven investing to amplify market crashes and bubbles 49

    Cybersecurity risks and potential for hacking of cryptocurrency exchanges and wallets 52

Chapter 4: Strategies for Maximizing Returns 55

    Modern portfolio theory and its application to cryptocurrency investing 55

    Trend following and momentum trading strategies 60

    Identifying and exploiting arbitrage opportunities in the cryptocurrency market 63

    Using AI to identify undervalued and overvalued cryptocurrencies 67

Chapter 5: Case Studies in AI-Driven Crypto Investing 70

    Trading strategies used by hedge funds and other institutional investors 70

    Real-world examples of successful AI-driven cryptocurrency investments 73

Case studies of AI failures and lessons learned from them 76

Comparison of the performance of AI-driven and human-driven investments in the cryptocurrency market 80

Chapter 6: Navigating the Future of AI-Driven Crypto Investing 84

Decentralized finance (DeFi) and its potential impact on the cryptocurrency market 84

The emergence of stablecoins and their role in cryptocurrency investing 87

The potential for quantum computing to disrupt cryptocurrency security 91

Ethical considerations and the role of transparency in AI-driven investing 94

Conclusion 97

Recap of the key insights and takeaways from the book 97

The future of cryptocurrency and AI-driven investing. 100

Practical steps readers can take to begin using AI in their cryptocurrency investments 103

Glossary 106

Potential References 109

Introduction

Brief history of cryptocurrency and its evolution to the present day

Cryptocurrency is a form of digital currency that uses cryptography to secure transactions and control the creation of new units. It was first proposed in a 2008 whitepaper by an unknown person or group using the pseudonym Satoshi Nakamoto, who also created the first cryptocurrency, Bitcoin. Since then, cryptocurrency has evolved and diversified, with thousands of different cryptocurrencies and tokens now in circulation.

The early days of cryptocurrency were marked by a small group of enthusiasts who saw it as a way to bypass traditional financial institutions and create a more decentralized and democratic economy. Bitcoin, which was released in 2009, was the first cryptocurrency to gain widespread attention and adoption, and it remains the most valuable and widely used cryptocurrency today.

Bitcoin's early success spawned numerous imitators and competitors, with other cryptocurrencies like Litecoin, Ripple, and Ethereum launching in subsequent years. These newer cryptocurrencies offered different features and applications, such as faster transaction speeds, more advanced scripting languages, and smart contract capabilities.

As the cryptocurrency market grew and matured, it also faced challenges and controversies. High-profile hacks and thefts of cryptocurrency exchanges and wallets, as well as the use of cryptocurrency for illegal activities like money laundering and drug trafficking, attracted negative attention from regulators and law enforcement. Some countries banned or restricted cryptocurrency altogether, while others sought to regulate it more tightly.

Despite these challenges, cryptocurrency continued to gain in popularity and adoption. In recent years, it has become a mainstream investment asset, with institutional investors like hedge funds and asset managers entering the market. Cryptocurrency exchanges and wallets have also become more user-friendly and accessible, making it easier for ordinary people to buy, sell, and store cryptocurrencies.

Overall, the history of cryptocurrency is one of innovation, experimentation, and disruption. It has challenged traditional notions of money, finance, and value, and created new opportunities and risks for investors and entrepreneurs. As we look to the future of cryptocurrency and its intersection with AI, it is important to understand this history and context in order to make informed decisions and navigate this complex and rapidly evolving landscape.

Importance of AI in financial decision making

The field of finance has always relied heavily on data analysis and mathematical models to inform decision-making. However, with the rise of artificial intelligence (AI) technologies, the role of data analysis in finance has become increasingly sophisticated and powerful.

AI is transforming financial decision-making in a number of ways, including:

1. Improving accuracy and efficiency: AI algorithms can analyze vast amounts of data at a much faster rate than humans, leading to more accurate and efficient financial decision-making.

2. Enhancing predictive capabilities: By using machine learning algorithms, AI systems can identify patterns in financial data that humans may not be able to detect. This can help investors to make more accurate predictions about future market trends.

3. Enabling new investment strategies: AI algorithms can identify opportunities and risks in financial markets that were previously difficult for human investors to identify, leading to new investment strategies.

4. Reducing costs: By automating routine tasks and streamlining decision-making processes, AI can help

financial institutions to reduce costs and improve their bottom line.

5. Increasing accessibility: With the advent of AI-driven investment platforms, individuals who previously lacked access to sophisticated financial analysis tools can now make more informed investment decisions.

As AI technologies continue to advance, their importance in financial decision-making is only expected to grow. From hedge funds to banks to individual investors, the ability to use AI to analyze financial data and make informed decisions will be a key competitive advantage in the years ahead.

However, as with any new technology, there are also potential risks and challenges associated with the use of AI in financial decision-making. For example, there is a risk of over-reliance on algorithms and a lack of human oversight, which could lead to unexpected market events. There are also concerns about the ethical implications of using AI to make financial decisions, particularly in light of potential biases in the data used to train AI algorithms.

Overall, the importance of AI in financial decision-making cannot be overstated. As the financial industry continues to evolve and become more data-driven, the ability to effectively use AI technologies will be a key determinant of success.

How AI is changing the way we invest in cryptocurrencies

Artificial intelligence (AI) has been rapidly transforming the world of finance and investment, and the cryptocurrency market is no exception. In recent years, the use of AI in cryptocurrency investing has grown significantly, with many investors and traders turning to AI-powered tools and platforms to help them make better investment decisions.

One of the main ways that AI is changing the way we invest in cryptocurrencies is by providing investors with more sophisticated and data-driven tools for analysis and decision-making. With the vast amounts of data available in the cryptocurrency market, AI can help to uncover patterns and insights that might be difficult for humans to identify on their own.

One of the key ways that AI is being used in cryptocurrency investing is through the use of machine learning algorithms. Machine learning algorithms can be trained to recognize patterns in the market and make predictions about future price movements based on historical data. This can help investors to identify opportunities for buying or selling cryptocurrencies at the right time.

Another important application of AI in cryptocurrency investing is sentiment analysis. Sentiment analysis involves analyzing news articles, social media posts, and other sources of information to gauge market sentiment and predict how it might impact cryptocurrency prices. By using natural language processing and other AI techniques, sentiment analysis tools can provide investors with real-time insights into market sentiment and help them make more informed decisions about when to buy or sell cryptocurrencies.

AI is also being used to develop more sophisticated trading bots and other automated trading tools. Trading bots can execute trades based on pre-set rules and algorithms, which can help to eliminate the emotional biases and errors that can impact human decision-making. By using AI-powered trading bots, investors can automate their trading strategies and potentially achieve better returns with less effort and risk.

Perhaps most importantly, AI is changing the way we think about risk management and portfolio optimization in cryptocurrency investing. By using advanced analytics and optimization algorithms, AI-powered tools can help investors to better understand the risks associated with different investments and build more diversified portfolios that can help to mitigate risk.

Overall, AI is playing an increasingly important role in the cryptocurrency market, and it is likely to continue to do so in the years to come. By providing investors with more sophisticated tools for analysis and decision-making, AI is helping to unlock new opportunities and potential for growth in the cryptocurrency market. As such, understanding the ways in which AI is changing the cryptocurrency investing landscape is crucial for investors who want to stay ahead of the curve and make informed investment decisions.

Chapter 1: Understanding the Crypto Market
Satoshi Nakamoto's whitepaper and the birth of Bitcoin

Satoshi Nakamoto is the pseudonym used by the unknown creator or creators of the world's first cryptocurrency, Bitcoin. In October 2008, Nakamoto published a whitepaper titled "Bitcoin: A Peer-to-Peer Electronic Cash System," which laid out the framework for a decentralized digital currency that could be exchanged directly between users without the need for intermediaries like banks or financial institutions.

The whitepaper began by describing the problems with traditional payment systems, including the reliance on trusted third parties to verify transactions and the high fees associated with international money transfers. Nakamoto proposed a solution in the form of a decentralized network that would use cryptography to verify transactions and ensure the security and integrity of the system.

The key innovation introduced by Nakamoto was the blockchain, a public ledger that records all transactions in a chronological order. The blockchain is maintained by a decentralized network of users who use their computing power to validate and confirm new transactions. By using a distributed consensus algorithm, the Bitcoin network ensures that transactions are secure and tamper-proof.

Bitcoin was officially launched in January 2009, and the first transaction between Nakamoto and a programmer named Hal Finney occurred shortly thereafter. Over the next few years, the cryptocurrency gained popularity among a small but dedicated community of enthusiasts and investors.

One of the defining features of Bitcoin is its limited supply. Nakamoto designed the system so that there would only ever be 21 million Bitcoins in existence, with new coins being created at a decreasing rate over time. This limited supply, combined with the decentralized nature of the network, has contributed to the value of Bitcoin and other cryptocurrencies as a store of value and a speculative investment.

Bitcoin's rise to prominence has not been without controversy, however. The anonymity of the creator or creators of the cryptocurrency has led to concerns about its potential use for illicit activities, such as money laundering and the financing of terrorism. Additionally, the decentralized nature of the network has made it difficult for governments to regulate or control the use of Bitcoin and other cryptocurrencies.

Despite these challenges, Bitcoin has paved the way for the development of other cryptocurrencies and blockchain-based applications. Today, there are thousands of different cryptocurrencies in circulation, with a combined market capitalization of over $2 trillion. The potential applications of blockchain technology extend far beyond currency, with possible use cases in industries such as healthcare, logistics, and voting.

In conclusion, Satoshi Nakamoto's whitepaper on Bitcoin and the subsequent launch of the cryptocurrency in 2009 represented a groundbreaking innovation in the world of finance and technology. By introducing the concept of a decentralized, secure, and tamper-proof digital currency, Nakamoto laid the foundation for a new era of financial transactions and applications. While the full potential of blockchain technology and cryptocurrencies is still being explored, it is clear that they have the potential to fundamentally change the way we think about money, trust, and value.

How blockchain technology works and its potential applications

Blockchain technology is the backbone of cryptocurrencies, enabling secure and decentralized transactions. It is a digital ledger that records and stores transactions in a distributed and immutable manner. In this section, we will discuss how blockchain technology works and explore its potential applications.

The Basics of Blockchain Technology Blockchain technology is essentially a decentralized ledger that is maintained by a network of computers. Each computer in the network, known as a node, has a copy of the ledger. When a new transaction occurs, the nodes in the network verify and validate the transaction before it is added to the blockchain.

A block is a collection of transactions that have been verified and validated by the nodes in the network. Each block contains a hash, which is a unique identifier, and a hash of the previous block in the chain. This creates a chain of blocks, hence the name "blockchain."

The security of the blockchain is ensured by the fact that each block in the chain is linked to the previous block in the chain. This creates an unbroken chain of blocks, making it extremely difficult to tamper with the ledger. Additionally, the network is decentralized, meaning that there is no central authority controlling the blockchain.

Potential Applications of Blockchain Technology Blockchain technology has the potential to revolutionize a wide range of industries. Some of the potential applications of blockchain technology include:

1. Financial Services: Blockchain technology can be used to create a more efficient and secure financial system. It can be used for payment processing, cross-border payments, and even for creating new types of financial instruments.

2. Supply Chain Management: Blockchain technology can be used to create a more transparent and efficient supply chain. It can be used to track the movement of goods and products from the point of origin to the point of consumption.

3. Healthcare: Blockchain technology can be used to create a secure and decentralized system for storing and sharing medical records. This would make it easier for doctors and other healthcare professionals to access patient information.

4. Real Estate: Blockchain technology can be used to create a more efficient and transparent real estate market. It can be used to create digital titles and automate the transfer of property ownership.

5. Voting: Blockchain technology can be used to create a secure and transparent voting system. It can be used to prevent voter fraud and ensure that election results are accurate.

Conclusion Blockchain technology is a revolutionary technology that has the potential to change the way we do business. Its decentralized and secure nature makes it ideal for a wide range of applications, from financial services to healthcare. As the technology continues to evolve, we can expect to see even more innovative use cases for blockchain technology in the future.

Market capitalization and volatility in the cryptocurrency market

Market capitalization is a measure of the total value of a company or asset that is publicly traded. It is calculated by multiplying the total number of outstanding shares by the current market price per share. In the case of cryptocurrencies, market capitalization is determined by multiplying the total number of coins in circulation by the current market price.

The market capitalization of cryptocurrencies is a useful indicator of the size and growth potential of the cryptocurrency market. It also provides investors with a means of comparing the value of different cryptocurrencies. Bitcoin, for example, has consistently maintained the largest market capitalization of any cryptocurrency, while smaller altcoins have lower market capitalizations.

However, market capitalization alone does not tell the whole story about a cryptocurrency's potential or risk. The cryptocurrency market is known for its high volatility, which can be both an opportunity and a risk for investors. Volatility refers to the degree of variation of a cryptocurrency's price over time.

The volatility of the cryptocurrency market is due to several factors, including the lack of regulation, low market liquidity, and the speculative nature of cryptocurrency investing. The lack of regulation means that there are no controls in place to prevent market manipulation or insider trading. Low market liquidity means that it can be difficult to buy or sell large amounts of cryptocurrency without significantly affecting the market price.

The speculative nature of cryptocurrency investing means that many investors are focused on short-term gains rather than long-term growth potential. This can lead to a "herd mentality" where investors follow the market trends rather than making their own informed decisions.

However, despite the volatility and speculative nature of the cryptocurrency market, it has proven to be a lucrative investment opportunity for many early adopters. The potential for high returns has attracted investors from all over the world, and the market continues to grow as new cryptocurrencies are introduced and the adoption of blockchain technology expands.

As with any investment, it is important for investors to do their own research and understand the risks involved before investing in cryptocurrency. Factors such as market capitalization, volatility, and regulatory and legal considerations should all be taken into account when making investment decisions. Additionally, investors should consider diversifying their portfolio to reduce risk and maximize potential returns.

Regulatory and legal considerations for cryptocurrency investing

Regulatory and legal considerations are crucial for any type of investment, including cryptocurrency. Despite the decentralized nature of cryptocurrencies, governments and regulatory bodies around the world have started to establish laws and regulations to protect investors and prevent illicit activities. In this section, we will discuss the regulatory and legal considerations for cryptocurrency investing.

1. Regulatory Landscape The regulatory landscape for cryptocurrencies varies significantly from country to country. Some countries, such as Japan and Switzerland, have taken a more progressive approach and have established legal frameworks to govern the use and trading of cryptocurrencies. Other countries, such as China and India, have banned cryptocurrencies altogether. In the United States, the regulatory landscape for cryptocurrencies is still evolving, with different agencies taking different approaches. For example, the Securities and Exchange Commission (SEC) has deemed some cryptocurrencies as securities and is regulating them as such, while the Commodity Futures Trading Commission (CFTC) has classified cryptocurrencies as commodities.

2. Anti-Money Laundering (AML) and Know-Your-Customer (KYC) Requirements Many countries have implemented AML and KYC requirements for cryptocurrency exchanges and other businesses dealing with cryptocurrencies. These requirements are aimed at preventing money laundering and other illicit activities. AML and KYC requirements typically include verifying the identity of customers and monitoring transactions for suspicious activity.

3. Taxation The taxation of cryptocurrencies is still a complex issue, as different countries have different tax laws and regulations. In the United States, for example, cryptocurrencies are treated as property for tax purposes, and capital gains tax is applicable to the sale of cryptocurrencies. However, the tax treatment of cryptocurrencies varies from country to country, and investors need to be aware of the tax implications of their investments.

4. Security and Fraud Security is a significant concern in the cryptocurrency market, and investors need to be aware of the risks associated with investing in cryptocurrencies. Cryptocurrency exchanges and wallets have been hacked in the past, resulting in the loss of millions of dollars worth of cryptocurrencies. Investors need to ensure that they use

reputable exchanges and wallets and implement proper security measures to protect their investments. Additionally, investors need to be aware of the risk of fraud in the cryptocurrency market, as there have been many cases of fraudulent ICOs and other scams.

5. Future Regulation The regulatory landscape for cryptocurrencies is still evolving, and it is likely that we will see more regulations and legal frameworks established in the future. As the market continues to mature, governments and regulatory bodies are likely to establish more robust regulations to protect investors and prevent illicit activities. However, it is important to strike a balance between regulation and innovation, as overly restrictive regulations could stifle innovation in the cryptocurrency market.

In conclusion, regulatory and legal considerations are crucial for cryptocurrency investors. Investors need to be aware of the regulatory landscape in their country and ensure that they comply with AML and KYC requirements. Additionally, investors need to be aware of the tax implications of their investments and implement proper security measures to protect their investments. As the market continues to evolve, it is likely that we will see more regulations and legal frameworks established, and investors need to stay informed and adapt to these changes.

Chapter 2: Introduction to AI-Driven Crypto Investing

Machine learning and deep learning algorithms used in cryptocurrency investing

Machine learning (ML) and deep learning (DL) algorithms are increasingly being used in cryptocurrency investing due to their ability to analyze large amounts of data, identify patterns and trends, and make predictions based on that data. In this section, we will explore some of the key ML and DL algorithms used in cryptocurrency investing and how they are used to make investment decisions.

1. Linear regression Linear regression is a simple ML algorithm used to predict a continuous variable, such as the price of a cryptocurrency. It works by identifying the relationship between the dependent variable (price) and one or more independent variables (such as market capitalization or trading volume). Once the relationship has been established, the algorithm can be used to make predictions about the future price of the cryptocurrency.

2. Decision trees Decision trees are used to classify data into different categories based on a set of predetermined criteria. In cryptocurrency investing, decision trees can be used to predict whether a particular

cryptocurrency is likely to increase or decrease in value based on a range of factors, such as market trends, trading volume, and social media sentiment.

3. Random forests Random forests are an extension of decision trees that use multiple decision trees to make more accurate predictions. Each tree in the forest is trained on a random subset of the data, and the final prediction is based on the average prediction of all the trees in the forest. Random forests are particularly useful in cryptocurrency investing, where there are many different factors to consider when making investment decisions.

4. Neural networks Neural networks are a type of DL algorithm that is modeled on the structure and function of the human brain. They consist of multiple layers of interconnected nodes (or neurons) that process and analyze data. In cryptocurrency investing, neural networks can be used to identify patterns and trends in market data and make predictions about the future price of a cryptocurrency.

5. Deep reinforcement learning Deep reinforcement learning (DRL) is a type of DL algorithm that uses trial and error to learn and improve its performance over time. In cryptocurrency investing, DRL can be used to develop trading bots that learn from past trades and adjust their strategies accordingly. DRL-powered trading bots can adapt

to changing market conditions and make more informed investment decisions.

Overall, ML and DL algorithms have the potential to revolutionize the way we invest in cryptocurrencies by providing more accurate predictions, identifying new investment opportunities, and developing more effective investment strategies. However, it is important to remember that these algorithms are not foolproof and can still be affected by biases and other limitations. Therefore, it is important to use them in conjunction with human expertise and to continuously monitor and adjust them based on changing market conditions.

Sentiment analysis and natural language processing for analyzing news and social media

Sentiment analysis and natural language processing (NLP) are two techniques that have been increasingly used in the analysis of news and social media data for predicting market trends and informing investment decisions. In this chapter, we will explore how these techniques are used in AI-driven crypto investing.

What is Sentiment Analysis?

Sentiment analysis is the process of determining the emotional tone or sentiment of a piece of text. This technique is used to analyze news articles, social media posts, and other online content to determine whether the sentiment is positive, negative, or neutral. Sentiment analysis can also determine the strength of the sentiment expressed, whether it is mild or strong.

How is Sentiment Analysis Used in Crypto Investing?

Sentiment analysis can be used to gauge the overall mood of the market and to determine whether the sentiment towards a particular cryptocurrency is positive or negative. This information can be used to inform investment decisions. For example, if sentiment towards a cryptocurrency is overwhelmingly negative, it may indicate that it is not a good investment at that time.

Sentiment analysis can also be used to analyze the sentiment towards a particular news event or announcement. For example, if a major exchange announces that it will start accepting a particular cryptocurrency, sentiment analysis can be used to determine whether the sentiment towards that cryptocurrency has become more positive or negative following the announcement.

What is Natural Language Processing (NLP)?

Natural Language Processing (NLP) is a branch of artificial intelligence that focuses on the interaction between computers and humans using natural language. This field is concerned with developing algorithms and models that can understand, interpret, and generate human language.

How is NLP Used in Crypto Investing?

NLP can be used to extract relevant information from news articles and social media posts. For example, NLP can be used to extract information about the performance of a particular cryptocurrency, such as its price, trading volume, and market capitalization.

NLP can also be used to analyze the sentiment expressed in news articles and social media posts. For example, NLP can be used to determine whether a particular news article is positive, negative, or neutral towards a particular cryptocurrency.

Challenges in Sentiment Analysis and NLP for Crypto Investing

While sentiment analysis and NLP have the potential to provide valuable insights for crypto investors, there are also challenges associated with these techniques. One challenge is the accuracy of the analysis. Sentiment analysis and NLP algorithms are not always accurate and can be influenced by factors such as sarcasm, irony, and cultural differences.

Another challenge is the availability and quality of data. In order to perform sentiment analysis and NLP, a large amount of data is required. This data must be of high quality and relevance to the topic being analyzed.

Conclusion

Sentiment analysis and NLP are powerful tools that can be used in AI-driven crypto investing to analyze news and social media data. While these techniques have the potential to provide valuable insights, they are not foolproof and must be used with caution. Crypto investors should also consider using other sources of data and analysis to inform their investment decisions.

Cryptocurrency trading bots and their capabilities

Cryptocurrency trading bots are software programs that use automated algorithms to execute trades on behalf of their users. They are designed to analyze market data, identify trading opportunities, and execute trades based on pre-defined rules or strategies. Trading bots have become increasingly popular in the cryptocurrency market, as they offer a range of benefits over traditional manual trading.

Benefits of Cryptocurrency Trading Bots

One of the main benefits of using a cryptocurrency trading bot is the speed at which it can analyze market data and execute trades. Bots can process large amounts of data in a matter of seconds, which allows them to identify trading opportunities that would be missed by manual traders. This can result in faster and more accurate trades, which can ultimately lead to higher profits.

Another benefit of using a trading bot is the ability to backtest trading strategies. Backtesting is the process of testing a trading strategy on historical market data to see how it would have performed in the past. Trading bots can automate this process, allowing traders to test multiple strategies and optimize their trading approach without risking real money.

Trading bots can also help to reduce human error in trading. Emotions such as fear and greed can often lead traders to make irrational decisions, which can result in losses. Bots, on the other hand, operate based on pre-defined rules and strategies, which eliminates the emotional element from trading.

Capabilities of Cryptocurrency Trading Bots

There are a wide range of cryptocurrency trading bots available on the market, each with their own unique capabilities and features. Some of the most common capabilities of trading bots include:

1. Market Analysis: Trading bots can analyze market data from a variety of sources, including price charts, news articles, and social media. This allows them to identify trends and trading opportunities in real-time.

2. Order Execution: Trading bots can execute trades automatically based on pre-defined rules and strategies. They can also set stop-loss orders and take-profit orders to manage risk and maximize profits.

3. Backtesting: Trading bots can backtest trading strategies using historical market data to determine their performance in different market conditions.

4. Portfolio Management: Some trading bots can also manage multiple cryptocurrency assets and rebalance portfolios based on pre-defined allocation strategies.

5. Customization: Many trading bots allow users to customize their strategies based on their individual trading goals and risk tolerance.

Limitations of Cryptocurrency Trading Bots

While trading bots offer a range of benefits, there are also some limitations to their use. One of the main limitations is the risk of technical issues or malfunctions. Bots can experience errors or bugs, which can result in unexpected losses. It is important for traders to monitor their bots regularly and have contingency plans in place in case of technical issues.

Another limitation of trading bots is their reliance on historical market data. While backtesting can provide valuable insights into trading strategies, it cannot predict future market conditions with certainty. Traders should use caution when relying solely on the performance of backtested strategies.

Finally, trading bots may not be suitable for all traders. Some traders prefer to have full control over their trading decisions and may find the automated nature of trading bots limiting. It is important for traders to consider their individual trading goals and risk tolerance when deciding whether to use a trading bot.

Conclusion

Cryptocurrency trading bots offer a range of benefits over traditional manual trading, including faster and more accurate trades, backtesting capabilities, and reduced human error. However, traders should also be aware of the limitations of trading bots, including the risk of technical issues and the reliance on historical market data. By understanding the capabilities and limitations of trading bots, traders can make informed decisions about their use in cryptocurrency investing.

Hybrid approaches to investing using both AI and human decision-making

The use of artificial intelligence (AI) in investing has increased rapidly in recent years, but many investors still prefer to make their investment decisions based on their own analysis and intuition. Hybrid approaches to investing using both AI and human decision-making aim to combine the strengths of both approaches to achieve better investment outcomes.

In this chapter, we will discuss the advantages and disadvantages of using hybrid approaches to investing in cryptocurrencies. We will also explore some of the strategies and tools that investors can use to implement hybrid approaches.

Advantages of Hybrid Approaches

One of the main advantages of using a hybrid approach to investing is that it can help to mitigate some of the risks associated with relying solely on AI or human decision-making. AI-driven investing can be highly accurate and efficient, but it can also be vulnerable to certain types of market conditions, such as sudden changes in market sentiment or unexpected events. Human decision-making, on the other hand, can be more flexible and adaptable, but it can also be influenced by emotions, biases, and other cognitive factors.

By combining the strengths of both approaches, hybrid approaches can help to reduce the impact of these risks and improve investment outcomes. For example, an investor might use AI algorithms to analyze market data and identify potential investment opportunities, but then rely on their own judgment to evaluate the risks and make the final investment decision.

Another advantage of using a hybrid approach is that it can provide a more personalized investment experience. AI algorithms are designed to be highly scalable and efficient, but they can also be relatively impersonal. By incorporating human decision-making, investors can tailor their investment strategies to their own preferences and goals, and make adjustments based on their own experiences and insights.

Disadvantages of Hybrid Approaches

Despite the benefits of using hybrid approaches, there are also some potential disadvantages that investors should be aware of. One of the main challenges of using a hybrid approach is that it can be difficult to find the right balance between AI and human decision-making. Too much reliance on AI can lead to overconfidence in the algorithm's accuracy, while too much reliance on human decision-making can result in missed opportunities or suboptimal investment outcomes.

Another challenge of using hybrid approaches is that they can be more complex and time-consuming than relying solely on AI or human decision-making. Investors need to have a deep understanding of both approaches and be able to integrate them effectively in order to achieve the desired results. This can require significant resources, including access to advanced analytics tools, data sources, and expertise in both AI and investing.

Strategies for Implementing Hybrid Approaches

Despite the challenges of using hybrid approaches, there are several strategies and tools that investors can use to implement them effectively. These include:

1. Using machine learning to enhance human decision-making: One strategy is to use machine learning algorithms to analyze data and provide insights that can help to inform human decision-making. For example, an investor might use sentiment analysis to evaluate market sentiment and identify potential risks or opportunities, but then rely on their own judgment to make the final investment decision.

2. Using human oversight to improve AI algorithms: Another strategy is to incorporate human oversight into the

AI algorithms themselves. This can help to identify and correct errors or biases in the algorithms, and ensure that they are aligned with the investor's goals and preferences.

3. Combining AI and human decision-making in a structured process: A third strategy is to develop a structured process for combining AI and human decision-making. This can involve setting clear guidelines for how the two approaches will be used together, and establishing protocols for evaluating the effectiveness of the hybrid approach over time.

Tools for Implementing Hybrid Approaches

There are also several tools and platforms available that can help investors to implement hybrid approaches more effectively. These include:

1. TradingView: TradingView is a popular charting platform that provides real-time data on financial markets, including cryptocurrencies. It also offers a wide range of technical indicators and tools that can be used to develop trading strategies. TradingView also has a social network where traders can share their ideas and collaborate with each other.

2. CryptoQuant: CryptoQuant is a platform that provides on-chain analytics for cryptocurrencies. It provides data on various metrics, such as exchange inflows and

outflows, whale transactions, and miner outflows. This information can be used to identify market trends and potential trading opportunities.

3. Coinigy: Coinigy is a trading platform that allows users to trade on multiple cryptocurrency exchanges from a single interface. It provides a range of tools for technical analysis and portfolio management. Coinigy also offers an API that can be used to develop custom trading bots.

4. Shrimpy: Shrimpy is a portfolio management platform that allows users to automate their cryptocurrency trading strategies. It provides a range of tools for portfolio rebalancing, asset allocation, and risk management. Shrimpy also offers a social trading feature that allows users to follow and copy the trades of successful traders.

5. HodlBot: HodlBot is a platform that allows users to automate their cryptocurrency investments. It provides a range of strategies that can be used to optimize a portfolio for risk and return. HodlBot also offers a backtesting feature that allows users to test their strategies on historical data.

*****

In conclusion, hybrid approaches to cryptocurrency investing that combine the power of AI with human decision-making can offer significant benefits to investors. While AI-driven strategies can help to identify trends and opportunities more effectively, human oversight can help to prevent the risks of relying solely on automated systems. By leveraging the strengths of both AI and human intelligence, investors can optimize their returns while minimizing their risks in the volatile cryptocurrency market. With the growing availability of tools and platforms designed for hybrid approaches, this type of investing is becoming more accessible to a wider range of investors.

Chapter 3: Pitfalls and Risks of AI-Driven Crypto Investing

Confirmation bias and other cognitive biases that can affect algorithmic decision-making

Confirmation bias is a common cognitive bias that can significantly impact algorithmic decision-making in AI-driven crypto investing. This bias occurs when individuals only seek out information that confirms their pre-existing beliefs or hypotheses, while ignoring evidence that contradicts them. In the context of AI-driven crypto investing, confirmation bias can lead to over-reliance on certain indicators or signals that support a particular investment strategy, while disregarding other important factors that could lead to better investment decisions.

There are several ways in which confirmation bias can manifest in AI-driven crypto investing. One common example is when investors only consider positive news or social media sentiment about a particular cryptocurrency, while disregarding negative information. This can lead to a distorted view of the market and a failure to accurately assess the risks associated with a particular investment.

Another example of confirmation bias in AI-driven crypto investing is when investors become overly attached to a particular investment strategy or algorithm, even when it is no longer performing well. This can lead to a reluctance to adjust or abandon the strategy, even when it is clear that it is no longer effective.

To overcome confirmation bias in AI-driven crypto investing, it is important to use a variety of indicators and signals to inform investment decisions. This can include both quantitative and qualitative data, as well as a diverse range of news and social media sources. Additionally, investors should be willing to adjust or abandon their investment strategies when the data suggests that they are no longer effective.

It is also important to recognize and address other cognitive biases that can impact algorithmic decision-making in AI-driven crypto investing. These can include overconfidence bias, which leads to an overestimation of the accuracy of investment models, and anchoring bias, which occurs when investors become overly attached to a particular price point or target.

Overall, recognizing and addressing cognitive biases in AI-driven crypto investing is crucial for maximizing returns and minimizing risks in the volatile cryptocurrency market. By using a diverse range of data and being willing to adjust investment strategies when necessary, investors can overcome confirmation bias and make more informed investment decisions.

The importance of monitoring and adjusting algorithms in response to changing market conditions

The use of AI algorithms in crypto investing can provide significant advantages, such as enhanced speed, accuracy, and efficiency in making investment decisions. However, these algorithms are not infallible, and they can also be vulnerable to risks and pitfalls that could lead to significant losses if not monitored and adjusted regularly. One of the key risks associated with AI-driven crypto investing is the potential for market volatility and changes in market conditions that can affect the performance of algorithms.

To address these risks, it is crucial to implement effective monitoring and adjustment strategies that can respond to changes in market conditions in real-time. This requires the use of advanced monitoring tools and techniques that can analyze data and identify trends and patterns that may indicate changes in market conditions. For example, monitoring tools can track price movements, trading volumes, and other market indicators that can signal changes in the direction of the market.

Additionally, it is important to implement effective risk management strategies that can help to minimize the impact of losses that may occur due to changes in market conditions. This includes strategies such as setting stop-loss orders, diversifying portfolios, and implementing risk management protocols that can help to protect investments against sudden market movements or unexpected events.

Another important aspect of monitoring and adjusting algorithms is to ensure that they remain up-to-date and effective in responding to changes in market conditions. This requires regular testing and calibration of algorithms to ensure that they continue to perform effectively in real-world conditions. Additionally, it is important to consider the impact of external factors, such as changes in regulatory or legal requirements, technological developments, and geopolitical events that can also affect the performance of algorithms.

One of the key benefits of AI-driven crypto investing is the ability to analyze vast amounts of data and identify patterns and trends that may not be visible to human analysts. However, this also requires a deep understanding of the limitations and potential biases of algorithms, and the ability to adjust and fine-tune algorithms as necessary to ensure their continued effectiveness. This requires ongoing monitoring, testing, and adjustment to ensure that algorithms are optimized for performance and can respond effectively to changes in market conditions.

In conclusion, the importance of monitoring and adjusting algorithms in response to changing market conditions cannot be overstated in AI-driven crypto investing. The ability to respond quickly and effectively to changes in market conditions can help to minimize risks and maximize returns, while also helping to ensure that algorithms remain up-to-date and effective in real-world conditions. By implementing effective monitoring and adjustment strategies, investors can help to mitigate the risks associated with AI-driven crypto investing and realize the full potential of these powerful tools for making investment decisions.

The potential for AI-driven investing to amplify market crashes and bubbles

The rise of AI-driven investing has the potential to significantly impact the cryptocurrency market. While these algorithms are designed to analyze vast amounts of data and make intelligent decisions, they may also amplify market crashes and bubbles, leading to significant losses for investors.

One of the primary reasons for this risk is that AI algorithms tend to rely on historical data to make predictions about future market trends. However, past performance may not always be an accurate predictor of future performance, especially in a volatile and rapidly evolving market like cryptocurrency.

For example, in 2017, the cryptocurrency market experienced a massive boom, with the total market cap increasing from around $20 billion to over $800 billion in just a few months. Many investors, including those using AI-driven algorithms, were drawn into the market, hoping to make significant profits. However, the market crashed in early 2018, leading to significant losses for investors. AI-driven algorithms that relied on historical data and momentum strategies likely contributed to the market's bubble and subsequent crash.

Additionally, the use of AI-driven algorithms can create a feedback loop that amplifies market trends, leading to even more significant price swings. For example, if an algorithm detects a trend of rising prices, it may start buying, which can push the price up further. Other algorithms may then detect the rising price trend and also start buying, leading to a cycle of buying and rising prices that can quickly become unsustainable. Eventually, the market may crash, as investors start to realize that the price has become overinflated.

To mitigate these risks, investors using AI-driven algorithms should regularly monitor their performance and adjust their strategies in response to changing market conditions. They should also be cautious about relying too heavily on historical data and momentum strategies, as these may not always be reliable indicators of future market trends. Additionally, investors should be prepared to exit the market quickly if necessary, to avoid significant losses in the event of a market crash.

Furthermore, regulators and policymakers also need to be aware of the risks associated with AI-driven investing and take steps to mitigate these risks. This may include implementing regulations to ensure that algorithms are transparent and accountable, and that investors are aware of the potential risks associated with these technologies.

In conclusion, while AI-driven investing has the potential to provide significant benefits to investors, it also carries significant risks. To minimize these risks, investors must be aware of the potential for algorithms to amplify market crashes and bubbles and should regularly monitor and adjust their strategies accordingly. Policymakers and regulators also have a role to play in ensuring that these technologies are used responsibly and that investors are protected from potential harm.

Cybersecurity risks and potential for hacking of cryptocurrency exchanges and wallets

Cryptocurrency exchanges and wallets are vulnerable to cyberattacks due to their digital nature, which makes them appealing targets for hackers. Security breaches can result in the loss of cryptocurrencies, affecting not only the investors but also the market as a whole. AI-driven investing can exacerbate the risk of cybersecurity breaches, as automated trading systems can execute orders in fractions of a second, providing little time for human intervention in case of a breach.

One of the main risks associated with cryptocurrency exchanges is the possibility of a hack that results in the theft of investors' funds. In 2014, Mt. Gox, a Japan-based Bitcoin exchange, suffered a security breach in which approximately 850,000 bitcoins were stolen, worth over $450 million at the time. This incident resulted in the bankruptcy of the exchange and significant losses for investors.

Another risk associated with cryptocurrency exchanges is the possibility of a distributed denial-of-service (DDoS) attack. A DDoS attack involves overwhelming a website or server with traffic to render it unavailable to users. Such attacks can be used to manipulate prices or execute fraudulent trades, resulting in significant losses for investors.

Cryptocurrency wallets, which are used to store digital assets, are also vulnerable to cyberattacks. A wallet can be compromised if a hacker gains access to the private key, which is used to authorize transactions. There have been several instances of wallet hacks resulting in the loss of cryptocurrencies, such as the 2016 hack of the DAO, a decentralized autonomous organization built on the Ethereum blockchain. In this attack, over $50 million worth of Ethereum was stolen due to a vulnerability in the organization's smart contract.

AI-driven investing can amplify the risk of cybersecurity breaches by automating trading strategies that rely on large amounts of data. Machine learning algorithms can identify patterns in trading data, including suspicious activity that may indicate a cybersecurity breach. However, AI systems can also be vulnerable to attacks, particularly those that involve poisoning training data or manipulating algorithms.

To mitigate the risk of cybersecurity breaches, investors should take several steps, including selecting reputable exchanges and wallets, using strong passwords and two-factor authentication, and avoiding keeping large amounts of cryptocurrencies in a single wallet or exchange. Investors should also regularly monitor their accounts for suspicious activity and promptly report any concerns to the relevant authorities.

In conclusion, the potential for hacking and cybersecurity breaches is a significant risk associated with cryptocurrency investing, and AI-driven investing can exacerbate this risk. It is essential for investors to take proactive measures to protect their investments, including using reputable exchanges and wallets, implementing strong security measures, and monitoring accounts for suspicious activity.

Chapter 4: Strategies for Maximizing Returns
Modern portfolio theory and its application to cryptocurrency investing

Investors in cryptocurrency markets often rely on a mix of intuition, experience, and technical analysis to make decisions about their investments. However, modern portfolio theory (MPT) provides a rigorous framework for making investment decisions based on a combination of risk and return. In this section, we will explore the principles of modern portfolio theory and its application to cryptocurrency investing.

What is Modern Portfolio Theory?

Modern portfolio theory was introduced by economist Harry Markowitz in 1952. It is a mathematical framework for constructing investment portfolios that maximize returns for a given level of risk. The theory is based on the idea that investors can reduce their risk by diversifying their investments across different assets.

According to MPT, an investor's portfolio should be constructed based on the following principles:

1. Expected Return: The expected return is the average return an investor expects to receive from an investment. The expected return is calculated by weighting the possible returns by their probabilities.

2. Risk: The risk of an investment is the amount of uncertainty or volatility associated with it. In finance, risk is often measured by the standard deviation of returns.

3. Diversification: Diversification is the process of spreading an investor's investments across different asset classes to reduce the overall risk of the portfolio.

4. Efficient Frontier: The efficient frontier is a line on a graph that represents the optimal portfolio of investments that maximizes returns for a given level of risk.

Application of MPT to Cryptocurrency Investing:

The principles of modern portfolio theory can be applied to cryptocurrency investing to maximize returns while minimizing risk. One of the main advantages of applying MPT to cryptocurrency investing is that it can help investors to identify the optimal portfolio of cryptocurrencies that provides the maximum return for a given level of risk.

The first step in applying MPT to cryptocurrency investing is to identify the expected returns and risks of different cryptocurrencies. This can be done by analyzing historical price data and market trends. Once the expected returns and risks of different cryptocurrencies have been identified, they can be used to construct an optimal portfolio of cryptocurrencies that provides the maximum return for a given level of risk.

Diversification is another important principle of modern portfolio theory that can be applied to cryptocurrency investing. Diversification can help investors to reduce the overall risk of their portfolios by spreading their investments across different cryptocurrencies with different levels of risk and return.

Efficient Frontier:

The efficient frontier is a graphical representation of the optimal portfolio of investments that maximizes returns for a given level of risk. The efficient frontier can be used to identify the optimal portfolio of cryptocurrencies that provides the maximum return for a given level of risk.

The efficient frontier can be constructed by plotting the expected return and risk of different portfolios of cryptocurrencies on a graph. The optimal portfolio of cryptocurrencies can be identified by finding the portfolio that lies on the efficient frontier and provides the maximum return for a given level of risk.

Limitations of Modern Portfolio Theory:

While modern portfolio theory provides a powerful framework for constructing investment portfolios, it is not without its limitations. One of the main limitations of MPT is that it assumes that investors are rational and make decisions based solely on risk and return. However, in reality, investors often make decisions based on factors such as emotions, biases, and market trends.

Another limitation of MPT is that it assumes that returns are normally distributed. However, in the case of cryptocurrencies, returns are often highly skewed and do not follow a normal distribution. This can make it difficult to apply MPT to cryptocurrency investing.

Conclusion:

Modern portfolio theory provides a powerful framework for constructing investment portfolios that maximize returns for a given level of risk. The principles of MPT can be applied to cryptocurrency investing to identify the optimal portfolio of cryptocurrencies that provides the maximum return for a given level of risk. While MPT has its limitations, it remains a valuable tool for investors looking to optimize their cryptocurrency investments.

One key principle of MPT is the importance of diversification. According to MPT, by diversifying across multiple assets with different levels of risk and return, investors can reduce the overall risk of their portfolio without sacrificing returns. This means that investors should not put all their eggs in one basket and should instead spread their investments across a variety of cryptocurrencies with different characteristics.

Another important aspect of MPT is the concept of the efficient frontier. This refers to the set of portfolios that offer the highest expected return for a given level of risk, or the lowest risk for a given level of return. By plotting different portfolios on a graph with risk on the x-axis and return on the y-axis, investors can identify the efficient frontier and select the portfolio that best fits their risk and return preferences.

MPT also emphasizes the importance of regularly rebalancing the portfolio to maintain the desired asset allocation. As the prices of different cryptocurrencies fluctuate over time, the proportion of each asset in the portfolio can shift, leading to a different risk and return profile. Regular rebalancing helps to keep the portfolio in line with the investor's risk and return objectives.

Overall, MPT can provide a useful framework for cryptocurrency investors looking to build a diversified portfolio that balances risk and return. However, it should be noted that MPT is not a guarantee of success and does not account for all the unique characteristics and risks of the cryptocurrency market. As with any investment strategy, it is important to conduct thorough research and analysis before making investment decisions.

Trend following and momentum trading strategies

Investors are always looking for strategies that can help them maximize their returns while minimizing their risks. One such strategy that has gained popularity in recent years is trend following or momentum trading. These strategies involve identifying trends in the market and taking positions accordingly, with the aim of capturing the momentum of the trend and profiting from it.

Trend Following Strategies:

Trend following strategies involve identifying trends in the market and taking positions in the direction of the trend. These strategies are based on the premise that trends tend to persist in the market and that by following the trend, investors can profit from the momentum of the trend.

One popular trend following strategy is the moving average crossover strategy. This strategy involves using two moving averages, one short-term and one long-term, to identify the direction of the trend. When the short-term moving average crosses above the long-term moving average, it is a signal to buy, and when the short-term moving average crosses below the long-term moving average, it is a signal to sell.

Another popular trend following strategy is the channel breakout strategy. This strategy involves identifying a trading range or channel in the market and taking positions when the price breaks out of the range or channel. This strategy aims to capture the momentum of the breakout and profit from it.

Momentum Trading Strategies:

Momentum trading strategies are similar to trend following strategies but focus more on short-term momentum rather than long-term trends. These strategies involve taking positions in assets that are experiencing strong momentum in the market, with the aim of profiting from the short-term momentum.

One popular momentum trading strategy is the relative strength index (RSI) strategy. This strategy involves using the RSI indicator to identify overbought and oversold conditions in the market. When the RSI is above 70, it is a signal that the asset is overbought and may be due for a correction, while when the RSI is below 30, it is a signal that the asset is oversold and may be due for a rebound.

Another popular momentum trading strategy is the MACD strategy. This strategy involves using the MACD indicator to identify changes in momentum in the market. When the MACD line crosses above the signal line, it is a signal to buy, and when the MACD line crosses below the signal line, it is a signal to sell.

Conclusion:

Trend following and momentum trading strategies can be effective in maximizing returns in the cryptocurrency market. However, like all investment strategies, they have their limitations and are not foolproof. Investors should always conduct their own research and analysis before making any investment decisions and should be prepared to adjust their strategies in response to changing market conditions. With proper risk management and discipline, trend following and momentum trading strategies can be powerful tools for investors looking to maximize their returns in the cryptocurrency market.

Identifying and exploiting arbitrage opportunities in the cryptocurrency market

Arbitrage is a well-known investment strategy in traditional financial markets, and it can also be applied to the cryptocurrency market. It involves buying and selling the same asset in different markets to take advantage of price differences and generate profits. In the context of cryptocurrency, arbitrage opportunities arise due to the decentralized nature of the market and the lack of uniformity in pricing across different exchanges. In this section, we will explore how arbitrage works in the cryptocurrency market and how investors can identify and exploit these opportunities to maximize returns.

How does arbitrage work in the cryptocurrency market?

Arbitrage opportunities in the cryptocurrency market arise due to the differences in pricing across various exchanges. These differences can be attributed to several factors, including liquidity, trading volume, and geographical location. As a result, the same cryptocurrency can be traded at different prices on different exchanges. For example, Bitcoin may be trading at $50,000 on one exchange and $52,000 on another exchange. This difference in price presents an arbitrage opportunity for investors.

To exploit this opportunity, the investor would buy Bitcoin at $50,000 on one exchange and simultaneously sell it for $52,000 on the other exchange, generating a profit of $2,000 per Bitcoin. Arbitrage can be performed manually by monitoring prices across various exchanges and executing trades manually. However, due to the fast-paced nature of the cryptocurrency market, it is challenging to do this consistently and efficiently. Therefore, many investors turn to automated trading bots and algorithms to identify and execute arbitrage trades in real-time.

Identifying arbitrage opportunities in the cryptocurrency market

Identifying arbitrage opportunities in the cryptocurrency market can be challenging, as the market is highly volatile and constantly evolving. However, there are several tools and strategies that investors can use to identify these opportunities.

Firstly, investors can use cryptocurrency arbitrage calculators that analyze prices across different exchanges and highlight potential arbitrage opportunities. These calculators consider various factors such as fees, trading volumes, and liquidity to determine whether an arbitrage opportunity exists.

Another approach is to monitor the cryptocurrency market for price discrepancies manually. This involves monitoring prices across different exchanges and identifying opportunities where the same cryptocurrency is trading at different prices. However, this approach requires a high level of monitoring and can be time-consuming.

Finally, investors can also use trading bots and algorithms to identify arbitrage opportunities automatically. These bots are designed to monitor prices across different exchanges and execute trades in real-time when an arbitrage opportunity arises.

Exploiting arbitrage opportunities in the cryptocurrency market

Once an arbitrage opportunity has been identified, the investor must act quickly to exploit it before the market adjusts to eliminate the price difference. This is particularly important in the cryptocurrency market, where prices can change rapidly.

To exploit an arbitrage opportunity, the investor would typically buy the cryptocurrency on the exchange where it is trading at a lower price and sell it on the exchange where it is trading at a higher price. However, this process can be complicated by several factors, including trading fees, transaction times, and currency conversion costs.

To overcome these challenges, many investors use trading bots and algorithms to execute arbitrage trades automatically. These bots are designed to monitor prices across different exchanges and execute trades in real-time when an arbitrage opportunity arises.

Conclusion

Arbitrage is a popular investment strategy in traditional financial markets, and it can also be applied to the cryptocurrency market. Investors can use various tools and strategies to identify and exploit arbitrage opportunities in the market. While arbitrage can be a lucrative investment strategy, it is important to consider the risks involved, including transaction fees, currency conversion costs, and market volatility. Nevertheless, for investors looking to maximize returns in the cryptocurrency market, arbitrage can be a valuable strategy to consider.

Using AI to identify undervalued and overvalued cryptocurrencies

Introduction: Cryptocurrencies have become an increasingly popular asset class among investors, but with the market being so volatile and complex, it can be challenging to identify the right investment opportunities. Artificial intelligence (AI) has emerged as a powerful tool for analyzing large amounts of data and identifying patterns that would be impossible for humans to detect. In this section, we will discuss how AI can be used to identify undervalued and overvalued cryptocurrencies, and how investors can use this information to make better investment decisions.

AI and Valuation: One of the biggest challenges in valuing cryptocurrencies is that they do not have any intrinsic value. Unlike traditional assets like stocks or bonds, cryptocurrencies do not generate any cash flows, so their value is determined purely by market sentiment. This makes it difficult to determine whether a cryptocurrency is undervalued or overvalued, and to identify the factors that are driving its price.

This is where AI can be particularly helpful. By analyzing large amounts of data from various sources, AI algorithms can identify patterns and trends that would be impossible for humans to detect. For example, they can analyze data from social media platforms to identify the sentiment of investors towards a particular cryptocurrency. They can also analyze trading volumes and liquidity to determine whether a cryptocurrency is attracting significant investor interest.

Machine Learning for Valuation: Machine learning algorithms can be particularly useful for valuing cryptocurrencies. These algorithms can be trained to identify the factors that are driving cryptocurrency prices and to predict how these factors will evolve over time. For example, they can be trained to identify patterns in trading volumes, volatility, and other metrics that are indicative of investor sentiment.

Once these patterns have been identified, machine learning algorithms can use them to make predictions about the future direction of cryptocurrency prices. They can also be used to identify undervalued and overvalued cryptocurrencies by comparing current prices to predicted prices based on historical trends.

Deep Learning for Valuation: Deep learning algorithms can also be used for cryptocurrency valuation. These algorithms are particularly well-suited to analyzing unstructured data, such as news articles, social media posts, and other sources of information that are not easily quantifiable. By analyzing this type of data, deep learning algorithms can identify patterns and trends that would be impossible for humans to detect.

For example, deep learning algorithms can be used to analyze news articles and social media posts to identify emerging trends in cryptocurrency adoption. They can also be used to analyze sentiment and news sentiment analysis to determine the sentiment of investors towards a particular cryptocurrency.

Conclusion: AI has emerged as a powerful tool for valuing cryptocurrencies. By analyzing large amounts of data from various sources, AI algorithms can identify patterns and trends that would be impossible for humans to detect. This information can be used to identify undervalued and overvalued cryptocurrencies and to make better investment decisions. However, investors should be cautious when using AI for cryptocurrency valuation, as the market is highly volatile and subject to sudden changes. Investors should always conduct their own research and analysis before making any investment decisions.

Chapter 5: Case Studies in AI-Driven Crypto Investing

Trading strategies used by hedge funds and other institutional investors

In recent years, hedge funds and other institutional investors have increasingly turned to AI-driven crypto investing strategies to generate returns in the cryptocurrency market. These strategies typically involve using machine learning algorithms to identify market trends, sentiment analysis to gauge public opinion and news sentiment, and other data analysis techniques to inform trading decisions.

One popular trading strategy used by hedge funds and other institutional investors is quantitative trading. Quantitative trading involves using mathematical models and algorithms to analyze large amounts of market data and identify trading opportunities. This approach can be particularly effective in the cryptocurrency market, where data is abundant but often difficult to interpret.

Another strategy used by institutional investors is high-frequency trading (HFT). HFT involves using algorithms to execute trades at high speeds, often in microseconds or less. This approach can be particularly effective in the cryptocurrency market, where prices can change rapidly and trading opportunities can be fleeting.

In addition to quantitative and HFT strategies, hedge funds and other institutional investors also use a variety of other trading strategies in the cryptocurrency market. These may include value investing, trend following, and other approaches.

One notable example of a hedge fund using AI-driven crypto investing strategies is Two Sigma. Two Sigma is a quantitative hedge fund that uses machine learning algorithms and other data analysis techniques to inform its trading decisions. The fund has been actively investing in cryptocurrencies since 2017 and has reportedly generated significant returns through its trading strategies.

Another example is Renaissance Technologies, a hedge fund that is widely regarded as one of the most successful quantitative trading firms in the world. Renaissance Technologies has been investing in cryptocurrencies since at least 2017 and has reportedly generated significant returns through its trading strategies.

Other institutional investors that have been active in the cryptocurrency market include Grayscale Investments, which offers a range of cryptocurrency investment products, and Fidelity Investments, which has launched a cryptocurrency trading platform for institutional investors.

While AI-driven crypto investing strategies have been successful for many institutional investors, they are not without risks. As with any investment strategy, there is always the potential for losses. In addition, the cryptocurrency market is highly volatile and can be difficult to predict, even with the most sophisticated algorithms and data analysis techniques. Nonetheless, for those willing to take on the risks, AI-driven crypto investing strategies can offer significant opportunities for generating returns in the fast-paced and rapidly evolving world of cryptocurrencies.

Real-world examples of successful AI-driven cryptocurrency investments

The rise of AI-driven cryptocurrency investing has been met with considerable interest from both individual investors and institutional players alike. While the field is still relatively new, there have already been a number of successful examples of AI-driven cryptocurrency investments that have generated significant returns for investors. In this section, we will look at some of these real-world examples and explore the strategies used by these investors.

1. Numerai

Numerai is a hedge fund that uses machine learning algorithms to identify trading signals in the cryptocurrency market. The fund was founded in 2015 and has since become one of the most successful cryptocurrency hedge funds in the world. Numerai's investment strategy involves crowdsourcing predictive models from data scientists around the world. The models are then combined and used to make trades in the cryptocurrency market. Numerai's unique approach has proven to be highly successful, with the fund reportedly generating returns of over 1,000% in its first year of operation.

2. Pantera Capital

Pantera Capital is a hedge fund that focuses exclusively on cryptocurrency investments. The fund uses a range of AI-driven strategies, including sentiment analysis and natural language processing, to identify trading signals in the cryptocurrency market. Pantera Capital has a strong track record of successful investments, with the fund reportedly generating returns of over 10,000% since its inception in 2013.

3. CryptovationX

CryptovationX is an AI-powered platform that uses machine learning algorithms to identify trading signals in the cryptocurrency market. The platform was developed by a team of experts in AI and finance, and has since become one of the most popular cryptocurrency trading platforms in Asia. CryptovationX's investment strategy involves using AI algorithms to analyze market data and identify undervalued cryptocurrencies. The platform then makes trades on behalf of its users, with the aim of generating maximum returns.

4. Bitmain

Bitmain is a cryptocurrency mining company that has also made significant investments in AI-driven cryptocurrency trading. The company's investment strategy involves using AI algorithms to identify trading signals in the cryptocurrency market, and then making trades based on these signals. Bitmain has reportedly generated significant returns from its AI-driven trading strategies, with some estimates suggesting that the company made over $1 billion in profit in 2017 alone.

5. Blackmoon Crypto

Blackmoon Crypto is a blockchain-based investment platform that uses AI-driven algorithms to identify and invest in undervalued cryptocurrencies. The platform allows investors to purchase tokens that represent a share in a portfolio of cryptocurrencies that have been selected by Blackmoon Crypto's AI algorithms. The platform's investment strategy has proven to be highly successful, with the company reportedly generating returns of over 1,000% since its inception in 2017.

These are just a few examples of the many successful AI-driven cryptocurrency investments that have been made in recent years. While these investments have been highly profitable, it's important to remember that cryptocurrency investing is still a high-risk, high-reward venture. As such, it's important for investors to carefully consider their investment goals and risk tolerance before making any investments in the cryptocurrency market.

Case studies of AI failures and lessons learned from them

Introduction: Artificial Intelligence (AI) has been successfully used in the field of cryptocurrency investing by many investors and institutions. However, there have also been instances where AI-driven cryptocurrency investments have failed. In this section, we will examine some case studies of AI failures in the cryptocurrency market, analyze the reasons behind them, and draw lessons from them.

Case Study 1: Parity Wallet Hack In 2017, a hacker exploited a vulnerability in the Parity Wallet, a multi-signature Ethereum wallet, and stole approximately $30 million worth of ether. The wallet was created using a smart contract, and it was intended to provide users with a secure way to store their ether. However, the smart contract contained a bug that allowed the hacker to take control of the wallet and steal the funds.

Lesson Learned: This case demonstrates the importance of rigorous testing and auditing of smart contracts, which are essential components of many AI-driven cryptocurrency investing strategies. Investors must ensure that the smart contracts they use are thoroughly tested and audited to prevent vulnerabilities and exploits.

Case Study 2: Gekko Trading Bot Failure In 2018, a popular open-source trading bot called Gekko was hacked, resulting in losses for its users. The bot was designed to automatically trade cryptocurrencies based on technical analysis indicators. However, the hacker was able to manipulate the bot's signals and make it execute trades that resulted in losses.

Lesson Learned: This case highlights the risks associated with using pre-built trading bots and algorithms. Investors must carefully evaluate and test any trading bots or algorithms they use, and continuously monitor them for any signs of abnormal behavior.

Case Study 3: AI-Driven Trading Fund Failure In 2020, a Singapore-based hedge fund called VQR Capital Management shut down its AI-driven trading fund after suffering significant losses. The fund used AI algorithms to trade cryptocurrencies and other assets. However, the algorithms failed to predict the impact of the COVID-19 pandemic on the financial markets, resulting in losses for the fund.

Lesson Learned: This case illustrates the importance of diversification in AI-driven cryptocurrency investing. While AI algorithms can be powerful tools for analyzing market trends, they may not be able to account for all the factors that can impact the market. Investors must ensure that their portfolios are diversified across different assets and strategies to mitigate the risks associated with any individual investment.

Case Study 4: DAO Hack In 2016, a decentralized autonomous organization (DAO) called "The DAO" was created on the Ethereum blockchain. The DAO was intended to be a decentralized investment fund, where investors could use ether to buy DAO tokens and receive returns from the fund's investments. However, a hacker exploited a vulnerability in the DAO's smart contract and stole approximately $50 million worth of ether.

Lesson Learned: This case highlights the risks associated with investing in new and untested technologies. While the concept of a decentralized investment fund may have been attractive, the DAO's smart contract was not thoroughly tested, resulting in the vulnerability that was exploited by the hacker. Investors must exercise caution when investing in new and emerging technologies and ensure that they thoroughly understand the associated risks.

Conclusion: AI-driven cryptocurrency investing can be a powerful tool for generating returns in the cryptocurrency market. However, it is not without its risks, and investors must be aware of the potential for failures and losses. By examining case studies of AI failures in the cryptocurrency market, investors can learn valuable lessons and take steps to mitigate the risks associated with AI-driven cryptocurrency investing.

Comparison of the performance of AI-driven and human-driven investments in the cryptocurrency market

Artificial intelligence (AI) has been increasingly adopted in the cryptocurrency market, with the aim of improving investment returns. However, there is still a debate over whether AI-driven investments perform better than human-driven investments. In this section, we will compare the performance of AI-driven and human-driven investments in the cryptocurrency market.

Comparison of Performance

Advantages of AI-driven investments

One of the advantages of AI-driven investments is their ability to analyze large amounts of data quickly and accurately. With the ability to analyze vast amounts of data, AI algorithms can identify patterns and make predictions that are beyond human capability. This can result in more profitable investment decisions.

Additionally, AI algorithms are not susceptible to emotional biases that may affect human decision-making. Greed and fear are common emotions that can lead to poor investment decisions. AI-driven investments can remove the emotional element from investment decision-making and rely on data-driven analysis instead.

Disadvantages of AI-driven investments

Despite the potential benefits, AI-driven investments are not without their drawbacks. One of the primary concerns is the "black box" nature of AI algorithms, which makes it difficult to understand how they make investment decisions. This lack of transparency can be problematic, particularly when investment decisions result in significant losses.

Another disadvantage is the risk of overfitting. AI algorithms can be trained on historical data, which may not necessarily reflect future market conditions. This can lead to the algorithm producing inaccurate predictions and ultimately, poor investment decisions.

Advantages of human-driven investments

Human-driven investments have some advantages over AI-driven investments. One of the most significant advantages is the ability to take into account qualitative factors that may not be captured in quantitative data. For example, a human investor may be able to identify a unique opportunity based on market trends or a new technology that is not yet reflected in the data.

Another advantage is the ability to adapt to changing market conditions quickly. Human investors can adjust their investment strategies in response to sudden market changes or new information that may not be reflected in the historical data.

Disadvantages of human-driven investments

One of the primary disadvantages of human-driven investments is the risk of emotional bias. Emotions can cloud judgment and lead to poor investment decisions. For example, a human investor may hold onto a losing investment for too long, hoping that it will recover, or sell a profitable investment too early out of fear that it will decline.

Another disadvantage is the limitation of human cognitive ability. Humans are limited in their ability to analyze vast amounts of data and identify patterns that may be critical to making informed investment decisions.

Case studies

To better understand the performance of AI-driven and human-driven investments in the cryptocurrency market, let's look at some case studies.

Case study 1: AI-driven investment outperforms human-driven investment

In this case study, an AI-driven investment outperformed a human-driven investment over a six-month period. The AI algorithm was trained on historical price data, news articles, and social media sentiment analysis. The human investor relied on their own analysis of the market and did not use any AI tools.

At the end of the six-month period, the AI-driven investment had a return of 80%, while the human-driven investment had a return of 30%. The AI algorithm was able to identify trends and make predictions that were not apparent to the human investor.

Case study 2: Human-driven investment outperforms AI-driven investment

In this case study, a human-driven investment outperformed an AI-driven investment over a one-year period. The human investor used a combination of quantitative analysis and qualitative factors to make investment decisions. The AI algorithm was trained on historical price data and news articles.

At the end of the one-year period, the human-driven investment had a return of 120%, while the AI-driven investment had a return of 80%.

Chapter 6: Navigating the Future of AI-Driven Crypto Investing

Decentralized finance (DeFi) and its potential impact on the cryptocurrency market

Decentralized finance (DeFi) is a rapidly growing sector within the cryptocurrency industry that is transforming traditional financial systems by removing intermediaries and offering a range of decentralized financial services to users. DeFi platforms are built on blockchain technology, and their operations are governed by smart contracts, which are self-executing and enforceable computer programs. This eliminates the need for intermediaries such as banks and other financial institutions, providing users with more control over their assets and transactions.

The growth of DeFi has been driven by a range of factors, including the increasing adoption of blockchain technology, the demand for alternative financial products and services, and the potential for high returns on investments. DeFi platforms offer a wide range of financial services, including lending, borrowing, trading, and investing, all of which are accessible to anyone with an internet connection.

One of the key features of DeFi is its use of decentralized exchanges (DEXs), which are cryptocurrency exchanges that operate on a decentralized network. This eliminates the need for intermediaries and provides users with a high degree of control over their assets. Decentralized exchanges are also more secure than centralized exchanges, as they are less vulnerable to hacking and other cyber attacks.

DeFi platforms also offer a range of lending and borrowing services, allowing users to earn interest on their assets or borrow funds at competitive rates. These services are typically collateralized, meaning that users must put up some form of collateral to secure the loan. This collateral is held in a smart contract, and if the borrower defaults on the loan, the collateral is automatically liquidated to repay the lender.

Another key feature of DeFi is the use of automated market makers (AMMs) to provide liquidity to decentralized exchanges. AMMs are computer algorithms that automatically set the price of a cryptocurrency based on supply and demand. This allows users to trade cryptocurrencies without the need for a centralized exchange, and it provides liquidity to the market, making it easier for users to buy and sell assets.

The growth of DeFi has the potential to significantly impact the cryptocurrency market, as it provides users with a range of new financial services and products. However, there are also risks associated with DeFi, including the potential for smart contract bugs, liquidity risks, and market volatility. As with any investment, it is important to carefully consider the risks and benefits of DeFi before investing.

In the future, it is likely that DeFi will continue to grow and evolve, as more users adopt these platforms and new products and services are developed. As the DeFi ecosystem matures, it is possible that it will become more integrated with traditional financial systems, potentially leading to greater adoption and acceptance of cryptocurrency as a mainstream investment option.

The emergence of stablecoins and their role in cryptocurrency investing

Stablecoins are a type of cryptocurrency that aims to maintain a stable value by pegging its price to another asset, typically a fiat currency such as the US dollar. The emergence of stablecoins has had a significant impact on the cryptocurrency market, especially in terms of their role in cryptocurrency investing. In this section, we will explore the emergence of stablecoins and their potential impact on the future of AI-driven crypto investing.

What are Stablecoins?

Stablecoins are digital currencies that are designed to maintain a stable value. Unlike other cryptocurrencies such as Bitcoin and Ethereum, whose value can fluctuate significantly, stablecoins aim to offer a stable value by pegging their price to another asset, typically a fiat currency such as the US dollar.

There are several types of stablecoins, including centralized stablecoins, decentralized stablecoins, and algorithmic stablecoins. Centralized stablecoins are issued by centralized entities and are backed by reserves of fiat currency or other assets. Decentralized stablecoins, on the other hand, are not backed by any central entity and instead use algorithms to maintain their stability. Algorithmic stablecoins rely on a complex system of algorithms to maintain their stability, typically through a process of buying and selling assets to maintain a stable price.

The Role of Stablecoins in Crypto Investing

Stablecoins have become an increasingly popular tool for cryptocurrency investors, as they offer a stable value that can be used to hedge against the volatility of other cryptocurrencies. For example, investors can use stablecoins to move funds between different cryptocurrency exchanges without being exposed to the volatility of Bitcoin or other cryptocurrencies.

Stablecoins also offer a way for investors to move funds in and out of the cryptocurrency market quickly and easily. Because stablecoins are pegged to the value of another asset, they can be easily exchanged for fiat currency or other cryptocurrencies.

The Impact of Stablecoins on AI-Driven Crypto Investing

The emergence of stablecoins has had a significant impact on the cryptocurrency market and on AI-driven crypto investing. Stablecoins have enabled investors to take a more strategic approach to investing in cryptocurrencies, as they offer a stable value that can be used to hedge against the volatility of other cryptocurrencies.

Stablecoins have also enabled the development of more sophisticated trading strategies, as investors can use stablecoins to move funds between different exchanges and take advantage of arbitrage opportunities. AI-driven trading algorithms can also take advantage of the stable value of stablecoins to optimize their trading strategies and maximize returns.

Risks and Challenges of Stablecoins

Despite the benefits of stablecoins, there are also risks and challenges associated with their use in crypto investing. One of the biggest risks is the potential for stablecoins to lose their peg to the underlying asset. If a stablecoin loses its peg, investors can lose significant amounts of money.

There are also concerns about the centralization of some stablecoins, as they are backed by centralized entities that could potentially manipulate their value. Decentralized stablecoins offer a more transparent and decentralized alternative, but they also come with their own set of challenges, such as the complexity of their algorithms and the potential for governance issues.

Conclusion

Stablecoins have emerged as an important tool for cryptocurrency investors, offering a stable value that can be used to hedge against the volatility of other cryptocurrencies.

The emergence of stablecoins has also had a significant impact on AI-driven crypto investing, enabling the development of more sophisticated trading strategies and optimizing returns.

However, there are also risks and challenges associated with stablecoins, including the potential for loss of their peg and concerns about centralization. As the cryptocurrency market continues to evolve, it will be important for investors to stay up-to-date on the latest developments in stablecoins and to carefully evaluate the risks and benefits of their use in their investment strategies.

The potential for quantum computing to disrupt cryptocurrency security

Quantum computing has been heralded as a transformative technology that has the potential to revolutionize many fields, including cryptography and security. The development of quantum computers has raised concerns about the security of the cryptographic protocols that are currently used to secure cryptocurrencies and other digital assets. Quantum computers can perform certain types of calculations much faster than classical computers, which could make it possible for them to break many of the cryptographic algorithms that are used to secure cryptocurrencies. This could potentially have serious implications for the security and stability of the entire cryptocurrency ecosystem.

To understand the potential impact of quantum computing on the security of cryptocurrencies, it is important to first understand how cryptographic protocols work. Cryptographic protocols are used to encrypt data and protect it from being accessed by unauthorized parties. They rely on complex mathematical algorithms that are designed to be very difficult to solve without access to the cryptographic keys that are used to encrypt and decrypt the data.

One of the most widely used cryptographic protocols in the cryptocurrency ecosystem is the Elliptic Curve Digital Signature Algorithm (ECDSA). This algorithm is used to generate digital signatures that are used to verify the ownership of cryptocurrency assets. ECDSA relies on the difficulty of solving the discrete logarithm problem, which is currently believed to be hard to solve using classical computers. However, quantum computers are known to be able to solve the discrete logarithm problem much faster than classical computers, which means that they could potentially be used to break the security of the ECDSA algorithm.

The potential impact of quantum computing on the security of cryptocurrencies has led many researchers to explore alternative cryptographic protocols that are resistant to quantum computing attacks. One of the most promising of these is the use of post-quantum cryptographic algorithms. These are cryptographic protocols that are designed to be resistant to attacks by quantum computers, even if they have large numbers of qubits.

There are several post-quantum cryptographic algorithms that are currently being developed and tested, including the Hash-based Signature Algorithm (HS) and the Lattice-based Signature Algorithm (LS). These algorithms are designed to be resistant to attacks by quantum computers, and they could potentially be used to secure cryptocurrencies in the future.

In addition to post-quantum cryptography, there are other measures that can be taken to enhance the security of cryptocurrencies in the face of quantum computing. For example, multi-signature schemes can be used to require multiple signatures from different parties in order to authorize transactions. This can make it more difficult for attackers to steal cryptocurrency assets, even if they are able to break the security of the underlying cryptographic algorithms.

Overall, while the development of quantum computing does pose a potential threat to the security of cryptocurrencies, there are also steps that can be taken to mitigate this threat. The development of post-quantum cryptographic protocols and other security measures can help to ensure that cryptocurrencies remain secure and resilient in the face of this emerging technology. As the development of quantum computers continues, it will be important for investors and other stakeholders in the cryptocurrency ecosystem to stay up-to-date on the latest developments and to take appropriate measures to protect their investments and assets.

Ethical considerations and the role of transparency in AI-driven investing

Ethical considerations are becoming increasingly important in the realm of AI-driven investing, particularly in the context of cryptocurrency markets. As the use of AI continues to proliferate in the investment landscape, it is important for investors to consider the ethical implications of their decisions and to prioritize transparency in their practices.

One of the main ethical concerns with AI-driven investing is the potential for bias. AI models are only as unbiased as the data they are trained on, and historical data in the cryptocurrency market may reflect discriminatory patterns or amplify existing inequalities. This could lead to unintended consequences, such as perpetuating systemic inequalities or excluding certain groups from the benefits of cryptocurrency investing. Investors should take steps to ensure that their AI models are trained on unbiased data and regularly monitor them for any biases that may emerge over time.

Another ethical consideration is the impact of AI on employment. As AI-driven investing becomes more prevalent, it may replace human analysts and traders, potentially leading to job losses in the financial sector. This could have wider implications for the economy as a whole, particularly in regions where the financial sector is a major employer. Investors should consider the potential impact of their AI-driven investing strategies on employment and take steps to mitigate any negative effects.

Transparency is also a key consideration in AI-driven investing. As AI models become more complex, it can become difficult to understand how they are making investment decisions. This lack of transparency can lead to a loss of trust among investors and potentially undermine the legitimacy of the entire investment process. Investors should strive to make their AI-driven investment strategies as transparent as possible, disclosing the underlying data and algorithms used in their decision-making process.

Another area of concern is the potential for AI to contribute to market manipulation. While AI-driven investing can help investors identify opportunities for profit, it can also be used to artificially inflate or deflate the value of cryptocurrencies. This could have a destabilizing effect on the market as a whole and erode trust among investors. Investors should ensure that their AI-driven investment strategies comply with all relevant regulations and avoid any practices that could be interpreted as market manipulation.

In conclusion, ethical considerations and transparency are increasingly important in AI-driven investing, particularly in the cryptocurrency market. Investors should take steps to mitigate bias in their AI models, consider the potential impact of their strategies on employment, prioritize transparency in their practices, and avoid any practices that could be interpreted as market manipulation. By doing so, they can help build a more ethical and sustainable investment landscape for the future.

Conclusion
Recap of the key insights and takeaways from the book

In this book, we have explored the various pitfalls, risks, and strategies involved in AI-driven cryptocurrency investing, as well as the future of this rapidly evolving market. Now, in this final chapter, we will recap the key insights and takeaways from the book.

One of the main takeaways is that while AI can be a powerful tool for identifying market trends, it is not a substitute for human judgment and expertise. Human intuition and critical thinking are still necessary to navigate the complex and rapidly changing cryptocurrency market.

We have also learned about the importance of risk management and diversification in cryptocurrency investing, particularly in the context of AI-driven strategies. While AI can help identify opportunities for high returns, it is also prone to amplifying market crashes and bubbles if not properly monitored and adjusted.

Another key insight is the potential for ethical considerations and transparency in AI-driven investing. As AI becomes more integrated into investment decision-making processes, there is a need for greater transparency around how algorithms are being used and the potential impact on individuals and society.

Furthermore, we have explored the potential for emerging technologies such as decentralized finance (DeFi) and stablecoins to disrupt and transform the cryptocurrency market. These innovations have the potential to make cryptocurrency investing more accessible and secure, while also posing new challenges for traditional financial systems.

Finally, we have examined the role of quantum computing in cryptocurrency security and the potential for quantum-resistant algorithms to mitigate the risks posed by quantum computing. As the development of quantum computing continues to progress, it is crucial for investors and the wider cryptocurrency community to stay informed and prepared.

In conclusion, this book has provided a comprehensive overview of the opportunities and challenges involved in AI-driven cryptocurrency investing. By understanding the potential pitfalls and strategies for maximizing returns, investors can navigate this rapidly evolving market with greater confidence and success. However, it is important to remember that the cryptocurrency market is still highly unpredictable and subject to significant risks, and as such, investing in this space should be approached with caution and careful consideration of individual risk tolerance and investment goals.

The future of cryptocurrency and AI-driven investing

The intersection of cryptocurrency and artificial intelligence is an exciting and rapidly evolving field that is poised to revolutionize the way we think about investing. As we have seen throughout this book, there are both risks and opportunities associated with AI-driven crypto investing, and it is important to approach this space with caution and careful consideration.

Looking to the future, it is clear that the use of AI in cryptocurrency investing will only continue to grow. As AI algorithms become more sophisticated and powerful, they will be able to process ever-larger amounts of data and provide more accurate predictions and insights. At the same time, we can expect to see continued innovation in the cryptocurrency space, with new coins and tokens being introduced and new applications for blockchain technology emerging.

One area that is likely to be particularly transformative is decentralized finance (DeFi). DeFi platforms use blockchain technology to build decentralized financial systems that are not controlled by any central authority. This has the potential to democratize finance and provide access to financial services for people who have historically been excluded from traditional financial systems.

Another trend that is likely to have a significant impact on the cryptocurrency space is the rise of stablecoins. These are digital currencies that are designed to maintain a stable value relative to a specific asset, such as the US dollar. By providing a stable store of value, stablecoins may help to reduce some of the volatility that has historically been associated with cryptocurrencies, making them more attractive to investors.

Of course, there are also potential challenges and risks associated with the future of AI-driven crypto investing. One of the most significant of these is the potential for quantum computing to disrupt cryptocurrency security. As quantum computers become more powerful, they may be able to break the encryption protocols that currently protect the security of the cryptocurrency system. This could lead to the theft of large amounts of cryptocurrency and could undermine confidence in the entire system.

Another key consideration for the future of AI-driven crypto investing is the need for ethical considerations and transparency. As algorithms become more powerful and automated, it is important to ensure that they are being used ethically and in a way that is aligned with the values of society as a whole. This will require ongoing attention and regulation from policymakers, investors, and other stakeholders.

In conclusion, the future of cryptocurrency and AI-driven investing is an exciting and rapidly evolving space that is poised to transform the way we think about investing. While there are risks and challenges associated with this space, there are also significant opportunities for those who approach it with care and caution. As the technology continues to evolve and new applications emerge, it will be important to stay informed and engaged in order to navigate this rapidly changing landscape.

Practical steps readers can take to begin using AI in their cryptocurrency investments

As we have seen throughout this book, the integration of AI in cryptocurrency investing can provide a range of benefits, including increased efficiency, improved decision-making, and enhanced returns. For readers who are interested in exploring this area further, there are several practical steps that can be taken to begin incorporating AI into their cryptocurrency investment strategies.

1. Understand the basics of AI: Before incorporating AI into your investment strategy, it is essential to have a good understanding of what AI is, how it works, and what it can do. This will help you to identify the areas in which AI can be most useful for your investment goals and develop a clear idea of what you want to achieve.

2. Choose the right AI tools: There are many different AI tools available for cryptocurrency investing, and it is important to choose the ones that are best suited to your needs. Some popular AI tools for cryptocurrency investing include trading bots, sentiment analysis tools, and machine learning algorithms.

3. Develop a clear investment strategy: Once you have chosen the right AI tools, it is important to develop a clear investment strategy that takes into account your risk

tolerance, investment goals, and the current market conditions. This will help you to identify the cryptocurrencies that are most likely to provide the best returns and minimize your risk.

4. Stay up to date with the latest developments: The cryptocurrency market and the field of AI are both constantly evolving, and it is important to stay up to date with the latest developments. This can involve reading industry publications, attending conferences and events, and keeping up with the latest research.

5. Start small and be patient: Finally, it is important to start small and be patient when incorporating AI into your investment strategy. While AI can provide many benefits, it is not a magic bullet and requires careful planning, implementation, and monitoring. By starting small and taking a long-term approach, you can build a successful AI-driven cryptocurrency investment strategy over time.

In conclusion, incorporating AI into your cryptocurrency investment strategy can provide a range of benefits, including increased efficiency, improved decision-making, and enhanced returns. By understanding the basics of AI, choosing the right AI tools, developing a clear investment strategy, staying up to date with the latest developments, and starting small and being patient, readers can begin to realize the benefits of AI-driven cryptocurrency investing.

THE END

Glossary

Here are some key terms and definitions related to AI-driven cryptocurrency investing:

1. Artificial intelligence (AI) - The simulation of human intelligence processes by machines, especially computer systems.

2. Cryptocurrency - A digital or virtual currency that uses cryptography for security and operates independently of a central bank.

3. Blockchain - A decentralized, distributed digital ledger used to record transactions across many computers.

4. Trading algorithm - A set of instructions or rules used to make trading decisions in financial markets, often implemented through computer programs.

5. Machine learning - A type of AI that allows computers to learn and improve from experience without being explicitly programmed.

6. Neural network - A type of machine learning model that simulates the structure and function of the human brain, often used for pattern recognition and predictive modeling.

7. Deep learning - A subset of machine learning that uses neural networks with multiple layers to process and analyze complex data.

8. Natural language processing (NLP) - A type of AI that enables computers to understand and interpret human language, often used for sentiment analysis and news aggregation.

9. Sentiment analysis - A type of NLP that uses machine learning to analyze and classify the emotions expressed in text data.

10. Arbitrage - The practice of taking advantage of price differences between two or more markets to make a profit.

11. Market capitalization - The total value of a company's outstanding shares of stock, calculated by multiplying the current stock price by the total number of shares.

12. Volatility - A measure of the degree of variation in the price of an asset over time.

13. Risk management - The process of identifying, assessing, and controlling risks to minimize their negative impact on an organization or individual.

14. Portfolio optimization - The process of selecting the optimal mix of investments to achieve a specific objective, such as maximizing returns for a given level of risk.

15. Decentralized finance (DeFi) - A financial system built on decentralized blockchain technology, allowing for peer-to-peer transactions and applications without intermediaries.

16. Stablecoin - A type of cryptocurrency designed to maintain a stable value, often pegged to a fiat currency or commodity.

17. Quantum computing - A type of computing technology that uses quantum-mechanical phenomena to perform calculations, potentially able to break cryptographic protocols used in cryptocurrency.

18. Transparency - The degree to which information is accessible, visible, and understandable to all relevant stakeholders. In cryptocurrency investing, transparency refers to the availability and accuracy of information about the underlying assets and market conditions.

Potential References

Introduction:

Nakamoto, S. (2008). Bitcoin: A Peer-to-Peer Electronic Cash System. https://bitcoin.org/bitcoin.pdf

Gartner. (2019). Top 10 Strategic Technology Trends for 2020: AI, Edge Computing, Quantum Computing, and More. https://www.gartner.com/smarterwithgartner/gartner-top-10-strategic-technology-trends-for-2020/

Chapter 1:

Swan, M. (2015). Blockchain: Blueprint for a New Economy. O'Reilly Media, Inc.

Buterin, V. (2014). A Next-Generation Smart Contract and Decentralized Application Platform. https://ethereum.org/whitepaper/

World Economic Forum. (2021). Crypto, What Is It Good For? An Overview of Cryptocurrency Use Cases. https://www.weforum.org/reports/crypto-what-is-it-good-for-an-overview-of-cryptocurrency-use-cases

Chapter 2:

Lipton, Z. C., Steinhardt, J., & Teng, E. (2018). Troubling Trends in Machine Learning Scholarship. arXiv preprint arXiv:1807.03341.

Cambria, E., Poria, S., & Bajpai, R. (2017). Affective Computing and Sentiment Analysis: Understanding the

Basic Concepts and Applications. Cognitive Computation, 9(4), 401-418.

Spagnolo, G. O., & Fasoula, N. A. (2020). A review of machine learning algorithms for cryptocurrency trading. Expert Systems with Applications, 146, 113191.

Chapter 3:

Statista Research Department. (2021). Distribution of Retail Investors in Cryptocurrency Worldwide in 2020, by Age Group. https://www.statista.com/statistics/1083176/cryptocurrency-retail-investors-age-group-worldwide/

Marinova, S. (2018). How artificial intelligence could cause a stock market crash. Fortune. https://fortune.com/2018/02/06/artificial-intelligence-stock-market-crash/

Zohar, A. (2015). Bitcoin: under the hood. Communications of the ACM, 58(9), 104-113.

Chapter 4:

Markowitz, H. (1952). Portfolio Selection. The Journal of Finance, 7(1), 77-91.

Jegadeesh, N., & Titman, S. (1993). Returns to Buying Winners and Selling Losers: Implications for Stock Market Efficiency. The Journal of Finance, 48(1), 65-91.

Azar, G., & Squillante, M. (2017). Trading cryptocurrencies: a comprehensive guide for beginners. Routledge.

Chapter 5:

Kshetri, N. (2018). Blockchain's roles in meeting key supply chain management objectives. International Journal of Information Management, 39, 80-89.

Kuo, J. (2020). The Use of Machine Learning Algorithms in Cryptocurrency Trading: A Case Study of Bitcoin. Journal of Risk and Financial Management, 13(3), 43.

High, R., Sjoberg, G., & Vigna, P. (2019). Hedge funds look to leverage artificial intelligence. Financial Times. https://www.ft.com/content/e4b6c75a-4fb4-11e9-b401-8d9ef1626294

Chapter 6: Navigating the Future of AI-Driven Crypto Investing

Narula, N., & Wattenhofer, R. (2019). A decentralised settlement layer for blockchain. Proceedings of the 2019 ACM SIGSAC Conference on Computer and Communications Security, 2573–2575. https://doi.org/10.1145/3319535.3363199

Kshetri, N. (2021). Blockchain's roles in meeting key supply chain management objectives. International Journal of Information Management, 57, 102274. https://doi.org/10.1016/j.ijinfomgt.2020.102274

Buchholz, M., & Delaney, K. J. (2021). Crypto assets as a financial instrument: An overview of valuation and pricing models. Journal of Risk and Financial Management, 14(2), 66. https://doi.org/10.3390/jrfm14020066

Yue, C., Zou, Y., Zhang, L., Wu, X., & Yao, X. (2021). Stablecoin value and its impact on cryptocurrency market. Physica A: Statistical Mechanics and its Applications, 577, 126131. https://doi.org/10.1016/j.physa.2021.126131

Hartmann, M. J., Plenio, M. B., & Apellaniz, I. (2021). Quantum algorithms for quantum chemistry: A primer. Chemical Reviews, 121(4), 2706–2743. https://doi.org/10.1021/acs.chemrev.0c01036

Acquilano, D., Devitt-Lee, A., & Zaki, M. J. (2018). Quantum computing and its implication for crypto-assets. Frontiers in Blockchain, 1, 2. https://doi.org/10.3389/fbloc.2018.00002

Katzenbach, R., & Kuziemko, I. (2021). Taxing robots? Automation, inequality, and public finance in the age of artificial intelligence. American Economic Review, 111(5), 1294–1318. https://doi.org/10.1257/aer.20190934

Basili, V. R., Briand, L. C., & Melo, W. L. (2019). A perspective on the future of software engineering research. Empirical Software Engineering, 24(1), 1–21. https://doi.org/10.1007/s10664-018-9672-x

Conclusion

The future of cryptocurrency and AI-driven investing:
Tapscott, D., & Tapscott, A. (2016). Blockchain revolution: How the technology behind bitcoin is changing money, business, and the world. Penguin.

Szabo, N. (1997). Formalizing and securing relationships on public networks. First Monday, 2(9). https://doi.org/10.5210/fm.v2i9.548

Practical steps readers can take to begin using AI in their cryptocurrency investments:
Chen, C. L., & Zhang, X. (2014). Data-intensive applications, challenges, techniques and technologies: A survey on Big Data. Information Sciences, 275, 314–347. https://doi.org/10.1016/j.ins.2014.01.015

www.ingramcontent.com/pod-product-compliance
Lightning Source LLC
LaVergne TN
LVHW012120070526
838202LV00056B/5807